A Crabtree Roots Book

FIREFIGHTER

DOUGLAS BENDER

People
I Meet

CRABTREE
Publishing Company
www.crabtreebooks.com

School-to-Home Support for Caregivers and Teachers

This book helps children grow by letting them practice reading. Here are a few guiding questions to help the reader with building his or her comprehension skills. Possible answers appear here in red.

Before Reading:

- What do I think this book is about?
  - *This book is about firefighters.*
  - *This book is about what a firefighter does at work.*
- What do I want to learn about this topic?
  - *I want to learn what a firefighter looks like.*
  - *I want to learn what a firefighter does.*

During Reading:

- I wonder why...
  - *I wonder why some people become firefighters.*
  - *I wonder why firefighters use helmets.*

- What have I learned so far?
  - *I have learned that firefighters help people and put out fires.*
  - *I have learned that firefighters drive firetrucks.*

After Reading:

- What details did I learn about this topic?
  - *I have learned that firefighters wear a helmet to protect themselves.*
  - *I have learned that firefighters use hoses to put out fires.*

- Read the book again and look for the vocabulary words.
  - *I see the word **firetruck** on page 6 and the word **helmets** on page 10. The other vocabulary words are found on page 14.*

This is a **firefighter**.

A firefighter helps people.

This firefighter is in a **firetruck**.

This firefighter has a **hose**.

All firefighters have **helmets**.

Do you know a firefighter?

Word List

Sight Words

a	in	this
do	is	you
has	people	

Words to Know

firefighter

firetruck

helmets

hose

28 Words

This is a **firefighter**.

A firefighter helps people.

This firefighter is in a **firetruck**.

This firefighter has a **hose**.

All firefighters have **helmets**.

Do you know a firefighter?

CRABTREE Publishing Company

People I Meet
FIREFIGHTER

Written by: Douglas Bender

Designed by: Rhea Wallace

Series Development: James Earley

Proofreader: Ellen Rodger

Educational Consultant: Marie Lemke M.Ed.

Photographs:
Shutterstock: Sergey Mironov: cover, p. 3, 14; Monkey Business Images: p. 1; Gorodenkeff: p. 5; Victor Moussa: p. 7, 14; Toa55: p. 8-9, 14; VAKS: p. 11, 14; Tyler Olson: p. 13

Library and Archives Canada Cataloguing in Publication

Title: Firefighter / Douglas Bender.
Names: Bender, Douglas, 1992- author.
Description: Series statement: People I meet | "A Crabtree roots book".
Identifiers: Canadiana (print) 2021017854X | Canadiana (ebook) 20210178558 | ISBN 9781427141149 (hardcover) | ISBN 9781427141200 (softcover) | ISBN 9781427133458 (HTML) | ISBN 9781427134059 (EPUB) | ISBN 9781427141262 (read-along ebook)
Subjects: LCSH: Fire fighters—Juvenile literature.
Classification: LCC HD8039.F5 B46 2022 | DDC j363.37/8—dc23

Library of Congress Cataloging-in-Publication Data

Names: Bender, Douglas, 1992- author.
Title: Firefighter / Douglas Bender.
Description: New York : Crabtree Publishing, 2022. | Series: People I meet - a Crabtree roots book | Includes index.
Identifiers: LCCN 2021014330 (print) | LCCN 2021014331 (ebook) | ISBN 9781427141149 (hardcover) | ISBN 9781427141200 (paperback) | ISBN 9781427133458 (ebook) | ISBN 9781427134059 (epub) | ISBN 9781427141262
Subjects: LCSH: Fire fighters--Juvenile literature.
Classification: LCC HD8039.F5 B46 2022 (print) | LCC HD8039.F5 (ebook) | DDC 363.37--dc23
LC record available at https://lccn.loc.gov/2021014330
LC ebook record available at https://lccn.loc.gov/2021014331

Crabtree Publishing Company

www.crabtreebooks.com   1-800-387-7650

Printed in the U.S.A./062021/CG20210401

Published in the United States
Crabtree Publishing
347 Fifth Avenue, Suite 1402-145
New York, NY, 10016

Published in Canada
Crabtree Publishing
616 Welland Ave.
St. Catharines, Ontario L2M 5V6